Navigating Change

Facilitating Change: Connecting People to the Change

Anjena Seewooruthun

Published by KDi Asia Pte Ltd

www.kdiasia.com
www.kdi-americas.com

ISBN: 10:9811123640
978-981-11-2364-1

Table of Contents

Preface

Chapter 1:	Introduction	1
Chapter 2:	Defining Change Facilitation	5
Chapter 3:	The Three Key Stakeholders and the Relationship Model	13
Chapter 4:	Achieve Win-Win Collaborations: *the Change Facilitator and the Project Manager*	25
Chapter 5:	Beyond Reporting: *the Change Facilitator and the Sponsor*	41
Chapter 6:	Engaging People in the Change: *the Change Facilitator and Middle Management*	59
Chapter 7:	Navigating Across Stakeholders	79
Chapter 8:	Living the Change: A Mantra We All Need to Embrace	89
Resources	Change Facilitator Requirements	95

Table of Figures

Figure 1 – KDi's Adaptive Path Framework	9
Figure 2 – KDi's Change Facilitation Model	10
Figure 3 – The Relationship Model	14
Figure 4 – Relationship Model Infographic	15
Figure 5 – KDi Change Analysis	30
Figure 6 – Building a Positive Working Relationship	38
Figure 7 – Trust Building Techniques	52
Figure 8 – KDi Organizational Perspectives	60

PREFACE

Audience

This companion book is aimed at those people in organizations carrying out a change management mandate when projects are implemented. They are often called change facilitators but at times this role is also carried out by project managers or integrated to an existing role such as communications executive or human resource executive.

I wrote this book to provide a helpful and practical resource as a toolkit for change facilitators. I felt that there was a need for a framework that guides and supports change facilitators in the planning and execution of the change management strategy.

This book offers an easily applicable model, which can be put into practice whatever the industry and whatever the project. It also highlights common pitfalls and obstacles that change facilitators face and how to navigate those challenges.

Acknowledgements

I would like to thank my husband Akshay and my parents for their unwavering belief and support.

My special thanks and acknowledgement also goes to:
Dr. Nancy Harkrider, change guru for her inspiring coaching and delightful friendship; Tan Kim Leng, whose creative pragmatism has provided me many insights and Jane Stackhouse, for her review.

CHAPTER 1

Introduction

When I was first introduced to the concept of Change Facilitator, I realized that there was actually a formal job title for this role that I felt I was already doing albeit in an informal and unstructured way. I was a project executive of the Program Office on a national modernization and reform project involving a big group of stakeholders. One of the things that I noticed within a month into the project was that the different work groups operated mostly in silos causing some form of information asymmetry. One of my tasks as project executive was to produce a synthesized weekly progress update report to the client/sponsor. As a result, I found myself in a privileged position of interacting with all project managers, middle management, end users and the sponsors.

I realized very fast that I was receiving much more information going beyond the formal progress update. Project managers informally talked of their constraints, concerns and pressures, which most of the time did not figure in their progress reports. Why was it not in their progress reports? Simply because these were people issues they were facing and from their perspective the report had to consist only of technical progress.

With the wealth of information I had, I soon realized that the project would face important challenges. But what could a project executive do? Without a change management mandate or the tools and techniques of change facilitation, it was extremely challenging for me to bring this alignment which I could clearly see was needed.

Nevertheless, I tried to be the connection point between the sponsors; the middle management-project managers; the project managers-end users and even to some extent the sponsors-end users. Although this role I was performing was highly informal, it quickly dawned on me that the sponsors and project managers valued these updates. I gained their trust and the ground information allowed them to get a better sense of issues. Similarly, the middle managers and end users often told me that it felt like I was their translator with project managers. In diverse contexts, speaking the same language does not lead to a common understanding. Having someone to bridge the gap and connect them enabled them to move forward.

It was at that point in the project that the change management component was activated and I was offered the Change Facilitator's position. I had the privileged of being coached by Dr. Nancy Harkrider and Tan Kim Leng, the managing directors of KDi Americas and KDi Asia. The KDi Change Facilitation Model and Adaptive Path Framework resonated deeply with me. Having been on the project and seen numerous change and people issues, I could see how change facilitation could really add value and help towards a smooth transition.

My entrance into the world of change management was one where I had already built relationships with stakeholders in the project and it made me realize how crucial these relationships were in helping me accomplish my role as change facilitator. In other change management engagements, which followed, I made relationship building with stakeholders a strong priority and leveraged on being the connection point to stakeholders to promote a much needed alignment to the future vision of the organization.

In this companion book, I propose a simple relationship framework to help the people involved in leading and facilitating change. This relationship framework provides an approach to navigate across strings of stakeholders to promote a smooth transition in any kind of change initiative. Whatever change facilitation methodology you use, you can apply it within this relationship framework. The relationship framework adds value at a broad level and will provide a much needed support when you plan and execute your change management strategy.

"We cannot change anything until we accept it."

Carl Jung

CHAPTER 2

Defining Facilitation Change

Overview and Benefits of this companion book

Organizations implement projects (e.g. IT modernization projects, launching of new products, opening of new branches) because of the intended benefits. However, simply executing the project will not lead to the expected benefits unless the change caused by the project is embraced and adopted by staff and external stakeholders.

To facilitate change is to enable people living the change to understand it, to accept it and to adopt it. A change facilitator puts people at the center of the change by focusing on how changes to systems, processes and technology impact people. This is done through the creation and implementation of a change management strategy and plan which seeks to maximize people's engagement and minimize people's resistance to enable a smooth transition.

This book recommends our relationship model that can be of tremendous help for change facilitators in working to drive adoption. By looking at the **relationship and interactions of change facilitators with project managers, sponsors and middle management**, the change facilitator is positioned across the chain of key stakeholders. Such a perspective will allow change facilitators to have a big picture view of the different pressure points. This is essential in enabling change facilitators to navigate more fluidly to bring an alignment among stakeholders for a smooth transition.

Structure of the book

Each chapter starts with an overview of key ideas and concepts introduced. Insights will be shared to strengthen your change initiatives. Some scenarios and case studies will be used as examples to demonstrate change facilitation strategies. Easily applicable strategies and tools have also been incorporated to guide you.

- The relationship model, which can strategically help you to navigate and lobby for needed support and alignment from stakeholders. (chapter 3)

- Change facilitators and project managers are two roles which should normally be well aligned. In practice, however, there are often divergences that lead to difficulties for the change facilitator to plan and execute a smooth transition. An understanding of these challenges and strategies to create win-win collaborations is proposed (chapter 4).

- With the sponsor, going beyond the traditional reporting to build a relationship of trust is an asset you can leverage for your change communication plan (chapter 5).

- Middle management, a group often neglected when considering priorities for relationship building, is identified as one of the critical success factors of Change Support Networks (chapter 6).

- Navigation skills support the execution of change facilitation plans. In fact, in addition to drawing the people centric change map, how you navigate your way on the map is also very important. Connecting stakeholders and ensuring that facilitating change is a joint stakeholder effort is equally vital (chapter 7).

- Living the change by seeing it as a constant is a perspective we must all adopt. To conclude the book, some reflections are shared (chapter 8).

Why Change Facilitation is an Essential Business Value

History is filled with examples of expensive project failures. While predominant in the public sector, the private sector is also not spared. Success of a project is traditionally measured by looking at the "iron triangle" of cost, scope and time but it makes more business sense to look at the success of a project based on the outcome it achieves. You might have a solution delivered on time , within budget and scope but if it is not used by people in the organization or does not perform the functions which the organization wanted, then it has failed. Successful projects are those which bring sustainable change in organizations.

There are different reasons and often a combination of factors that explain why projects fail. Lack of communication, lack of ownership and failure to engage those who will ultimately use the new system are often cited in the post implementation review. Change facilitation cannot resolve every problem which led a project to fail but it can certainly address the key ones I have described. Focusing on people and putting them at the center of any change initiative can achieve sustainable change. A change facilitation strategy, that includes a change communication and an engagement plan, provides a way of ensuring people are not forgotten.

Change facilitation will also ensure that the stakeholders are able to visualize their future by articulating the changes and their impacts . Without this, stakeholders initially only see the project as the organization's strategy and plan with objectives and benefits. As they start to realize that the changes in their organization will impact their role and daily operations, uncertainty often quickly settles in. If not addressed, such uncertainties can fuel rumors and fear leading to an environment of distrust which is very detrimental to the organization.

"The competition for knowledge workers and cost of turnover is a critical issue. People-centered change is the only proactive approach to engage and retain skilled workers."-Jane Stackhouse, Consultant and former Nike HR Portfolio Training

The *Leading Change that Matters* [1] (LCtM) book offers a much-needed perspective for embarking on sustainable change. Based on client engagements across a diversity of countries, the LCtM book is a valuable resource on effectively leading change. If you are a change facilitator or senior management championing change projects, it is recommended that you read it as it provides important notions of "the how and why" of people-centered change along with holistic change planning methods and implementation strategies tested on the ground.

The LCtM book shares KDi's Change Facilitation Model that follows to lead people-centric change in organizations. The four stage communication model includes:

- "Reframe Change" stage which addresses entrenched mindsets, challenges in the way we think about change and the need to recognize change as a constant.
- "Plan Change" highlights the need to assess people's readiness to change, to map the change which is happening and its impact.
- "Implement Change" includes the Adaptive Path Framework (see Figure 1 on page 9) – the need to create awareness,

---

[1] Dr. Nancy Harkrider and Tan Kim Leng (2013): Leading Change that Matters: Making Adoption a Reality, 1st edition, KDI Asia Pte Ltd.

cultivate acceptance and facilitate adoption of the changes. The awareness phase is about explaining and defining the change initiative: answering the simple but important question of what the project is all about. The acceptance phase describes the changes and benefits to the people undergoing the change. The adoption phase is about participation and action oriented involvement of people.

- "Navigate Change" covers the need to sustain changes that organizations have implemented, providing an understanding that change is continuous.

Encourage and Navigate Change

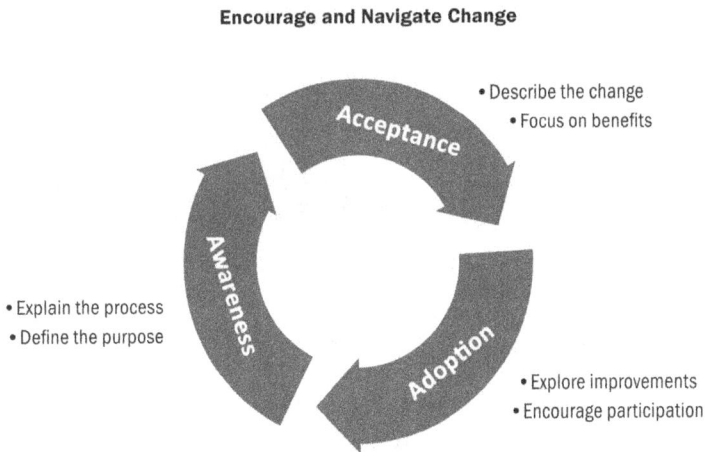

• Describe the change
• Focus on benefits

• Explain the process
• Define the purpose

• Explore improvements
• Encourage participation

Figure 1 - KDi's Adaptive Path Framewok

People are drivers of change in an organization

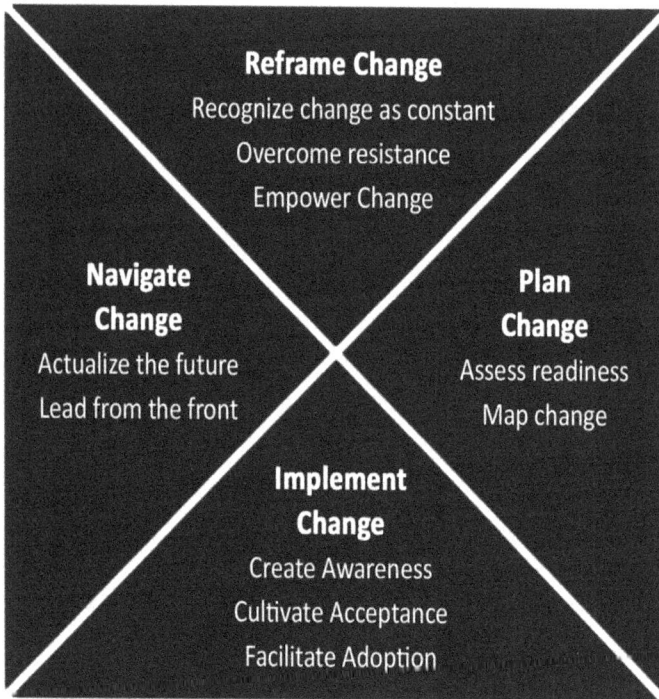

Reframe Change
Recognize change as constant
Overcome resistance
Empower Change

Navigate Change
Actualize the future
Lead from the front

Plan Change
Assess readiness
Map change

Implement Change
Create Awareness
Cultivate Acceptance
Facilitate Adoption

The leadership role changes in each phase of the model

Figure 2 - KDi's Change Facilitation Model

Set within the KDi's Change Facilitation Model, this companion book proposes a relationship framework for how change facilitators can best navigate across projects' stakeholders to implement the change management plans. The relationship model is built around the different essential relationships of the change facilitator. It is crucial that you understand how to manage and navigate across sponsors, middle management and project managers. As a change facilitator, you will work to drive adoption of the changes caused by a project. If you build solid working relationships with your key stakeholders you can then rely on the relationship model for support in executing their plans.

An important point to note is that positions of authority are not always synonymous to positions to influence. This is why in many projects, stakeholders in positions of authority may not succeed in influencing staff to overcome their concerns and resistance to change. Facilitating change involves the ability to influence and to gather momentum for change among stakeholders. However, the support of those in positions of authority are not to be neglected. By navigating across stakeholders (in both positions of authority and influence) and building a relationship of trust with them, you will be able to act as the connection point among them. The resulting aligned mindset will enable you to engage them in facilitating change in the organization.

"Achieving awareness, acceptance and ultimately adoption is only possible through winning the hearts and minds of stakeholders."

Dr. Nancy Harkrider and Tan Kim Leng

"All is connected ... no one thing can change by itself."

Paul Hawken

The Three Key Stakeholders and the Relationship Model

Overview

There are always many groups of stakeholders with different interests and pressure points which need to be considered when facilitating change within an organization. There are internal stakeholders - the people within the different layers of the organization: the leaders, the middle managers and the staff. Equally important are the external stakeholders – people outside the organization who will be impacted by a change within the organization. For example in the case of implementation of new IT systems and centralized reporting of a central bank, the internal stakeholders are the departments within the central bank affected and the external stakeholders are the credit institutions impacted.

This book focuses on three key groups of stakeholders - the project manager(s), the sponsor and the middle managers. It proposes a relationship framework that will help you as a change facilitator apply and execute your different change management strategies and techniques.

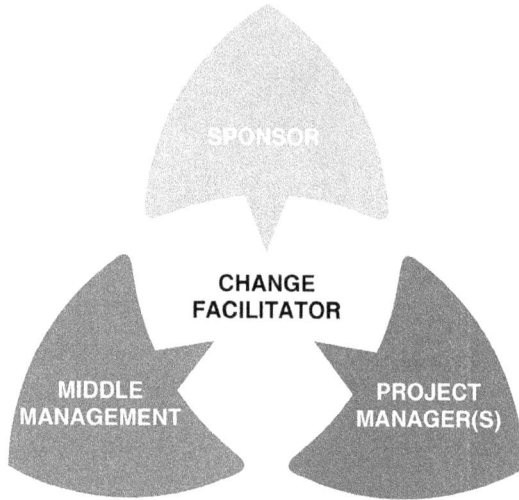

Figure 3 - The Relationship Model

The relationship model forces you to take a step back and visualize the interaction of these three groups of stakeholders with each other and with the change facilitator. For example, when planning for change, the change facilitator will start connecting with these different stakeholders to understand the project, the changes and their impact. Similarly, when implementing change and carrying out activities across the awareness, acceptance and adoption phase, the change facilitator will be in a uniquely privileged position to understand the challenges and concerns of the sponsor, project manager middle management and end users.

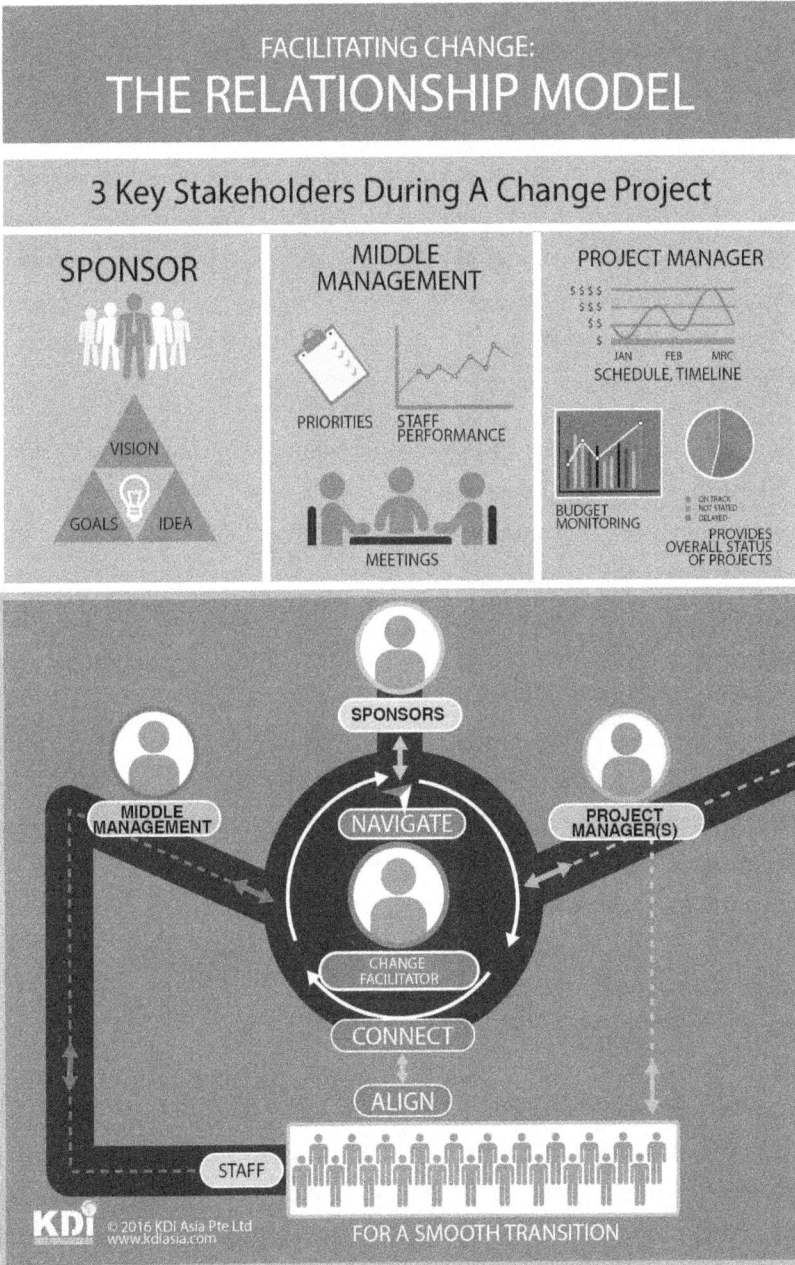

Figure 4 – Relationship Model Infographic

This model stems from the nature of the role of a change facilitator, who in working for a smooth transition interacts closely with the sponsor, the middle managers and the project manager(s). Such interactions position the change facilitator as a key connection point having the capacity to foresee many stumbling blocks of projects and bringing an often necessary alignment among these three stakeholder groups. Therefore, setting your change management methodology within the relationship model will guide you in having an approach which yields results.

The relationship model is based on building a strong rapport with each of the three key stakeholder groups. In spite of the advantageous position that a change facilitator can be in, the ability to connect, align and navigate among the stakeholders will depend heavily on the strength of the relationship which exists between the change facilitator and each of these four stakeholders. The next chapters cover some strategies for building strong and resilient relationships. Beyond building a relationship of trust with these three stakeholder groups, the relationship model is about integrating the various change management strategies within your interaction with these stakeholders. This is how you can serve as a connection point which empowers alignment.

Why are relationships essential ?

Relationships are essential as they are the conduit to sharing the meaning of what change in the work place represents for different groups of stakeholders. As a change facilitator you can understand the change happening, you can have a set of effective strategies and tools but without the relationship aspect, you will struggle to understand the roots of concerns and resistance from the different parties. The relationship approach is also the glue which allows you to connect to the three essential stakeholders.

Project Managers

Within the organization, some of the internal stakeholders may be directly involved in driving the change initiative. This would often be the core project implementation team, led by one or several project managers. Often in cases of IT modernization projects, the project manager is an outsourced component, coming from another organization, to work with the internal core team to deliver an upgraded IT infrastructure. In such cases, the internal project managers and the outsourced project managers may not be closely aligned. Gaps often exist between these two parties and often change facilitators who are simply doing their job to uncover and address concerns of staff within the organization may suddenly find themselves caught between these two groups of stakeholders. Your relationship with both parties can help you add value by bringing them to focus on the future vision of the organization and how to get there with the changes being implemented.

Sponsors

At the head of organizations are the leaders who see the big picture and need results to showcase improvements as a result of changes implemented. It is easy to only think of your relationship with a sponsor as one solely focused on reporting. While it is true that sponsors will want status updates and progress reports, building your relationship with the sponsors will enable you to have a voice in strategically driving adoption.

Sponsors play a key role in change management as they have the influence over staff and can lead their people to believe in and embrace changes. To achieve that, they need to be visible, engage with staff and consider managing the people side of change as a priority. The degree to which sponsors understand change management varies. That means that as a change facilitator you cannot assume that just because you have a role in a particular change initiative that your role and its value-add is understood.

In many projects, sponsors are more focused on the project managers' deliverables – the tangibles. Sponsors have their own reporting hierarchy and they will need to demonstrate that the change initiative they are leading is on the right track and will yield results. They will often focus on keeping track of the project schedule and the budget. You will need to be able to demonstrate to the sponsor that your role is crucial. An important yet tricky part of your relationship with the sponsor will be to be able to assess their level of understanding change management and, where needed you will have to consolidate their knowledge to ensure they understand that change is a process which is facilitated by all stakeholders.

Middle managers and the Change Support Network

Another group of key internal stakeholders are the middle managers who are the gate keepers for accessing end users/front line staff. In focusing on the sponsor relationship, which represents the high level management, engagement with middle managers is often overlooked. However, middle managers who have the trust of both their subordinates and superiors are a critical group for the change facilitator to engage with as they can significantly drive adoption.

In general, end users are the group most impacted by change. As a change facilitator you will not be able to speak to each and every staff, which is why you will want to have a Change Support Network established. A Change Support Network (CSN) is a group of carefully selected stakeholders from different departments who have the trust of both staff and upper management. They will assist you and your team in communicating the project, but most importantly, they will provide you with a pulse from the ground up. Middle managers can be part of the Change Support Network but they generally appoint team leaders or key staff.

To establish and gain the trust of the CSN, a relationship approach is essential. The CSN can make a major difference in how fast end-users adopt new systems and way of work. Before this happens, buy-in from the middle managers must be secured. It is important to realize that the internal project managers implementing the change initiative and middle managers may have different views as well as different understanding of what the change is or what the change should be, even if both parties belong inside the organization. The change facilitator can contribute to a needed alignment by leveraging on her position as connecting point.

Using this knowledge to strengthen change initiatives

You can use the relationship approach in any type of change initiative. While the idea of a relationship with each groups of stakeholders seems simple enough, the challenge comes from the fact that it takes time and effort to build relationships and that people are all different with different levels of influence, power and having complex behaviors. Change facilitators must be able to deal with different power relationships without wavering from their integrity and the job they have been hired to do.

CHAPTER 3: THE THREE KEY STAKEHOLDERS AND THE RELATIONSHIP MODEL

"More than any other job function, Change Facilitators must hold to their passions for what matters. That's the only way they won't burn out."

- Dr. Nancy Harkrider

The key to strengthening your abilities in facilitating change is in applying your change management techniques and tools through this relationship model. The next three chapters will go into detail on the "how" part – how to build relationships and become the key connection point, how to navigate across these stakeholders to bring a necessary alignment and smooth transition. They will also cover some of the techniques when planning and when implementing change. These will be combined with the relationship approach to demonstrate how you can use this knowledge to make more impact as a change facilitator.

The relationship model becomes even more essential when working on change projects in countries that are new to the concepts of change management. Development trends show that both public and private sector in developing countries are more and more focused on technology, automation and process improvement. This means a lot of significant changes with a crucial need for adopting these changes for the country to be able to move ahead. Therefore, it is not surprising that the advisory part, when the project is being decided on, will strongly recommend a change management portion.

Similarly, significant change projects funded by international donor organizations will often require that the project implementation include change management. This stems from lessons learned from failed projects where new technology implemented worked but people never used the new systems. While it is a key step forward in the development world to require change management in projects, just having that component in projects gives no guarantees.

As a change facilitator in a situation where your client organization is new to change management, how do you get the decision makers to move away from having a tick-the-box approach with change management? How do you get your stakeholders to trust you and to believe in the benefits that change management can bring? If you dive directly into planning for the change, you will very quickly hit stumbling blocks as you start engaging with stakeholders who do not understand your value add.

Start by building your relationship with your stakeholders and leverage on it to get buy-in. Spend some time getting to know the different groups of stakeholders and understanding their interests and concerns, demonstrating how you can facilitate the transition. When planning for change for example, you will want to ensure that your change management activities and deliverables are integrated in the master project plan. This will enable the project manager(s) as well as the sponsor to see the overall picture of how the people side and the new technology/systems side fit in together. It will also clearly show the importance of correctly sequencing change management activities . However, some project manager(s) might be reluctant to include the "soft" side of the project in their schedule especially if seen to have possible impacts on timeline.

By using the relationship approach and sharing with the project manager(s) how your role can support implementation, they will be less inclined to refuse you. You need to be constantly lobbying to ensure your voice is heard. This will ensure your recommendations are listened to and you are able to execute your change management mandate. Similarly with the CSN, depending on the context of the country and organization in which you are operating, you may find it

hard to have a formal CSN in place. However, with the relationships
that you develop with middle managers and end users/staff, you may
have an informal CSN and get the relevant ground information which
you need.

The relationship model allows you to see the interests, constraints
and concerns of the different groups from different perspectives. It
further positions you in the strategic position of being the connection
point to these different stakeholders. In addition to your change
management tools and techniques, strong relationships and the trust
which you manage to build with the different stakeholder groups will
enable you to lead a smooth transition in any change initiative.

"No one can whistle a symphony. It takes a whole orchestra to play it."

H.E. Luccock

CHAPTER 4

Achieve Win-win Collaborations

The Change Facilitator and the Project Manager

Overview

There are always people who you will find it challenging to work with because they operate from a very different frame of mind than yours. It cannot be avoided but it is important to keep an open mind and remember that we are all unique individuals with something to offer. Project managers and change facilitators will often find themselves approaching issues very differently but this is not necessarily a bad thing if both parties are self-aware and focus on resolving issues with a win-win approach. Such an approach will reap benefits as the two stakeholder groups can complement each other with different perspective and knowledge.

This chapter will explore some of the typical divergences between project managers and change facilitators, highlighting how it can impede on the change initiative. Using the relationship approach, however, a change facilitator can work towards better collaboration with the project manager. The benefits for change facilitators in having built a positive relationship with the project manager are very high. Change facilitators will be more effective in executing their mandate.

The result of a positive relationship will be a stronger team working all the angles for a smooth transition.

The Change Facilitator and the Project Manager

When you are facilitating change in any type of initiative, the project manager will represent one of your key stakeholders. It is easy to forget about managing the relationship with the project manager and focus only on the sponsor, change support network and end users. However, it is essential to look at the project manager as a stakeholder with whom you need to build the right foundations from the start of the project. Both of you will also need to continuously touch base in order to keep a close alignment.

Different focus and priorities

The change facilitator and project manager roles have different focuses. While the change facilitator's main concern will be on people issues, the project manager will have the project content/scope, schedule and cost as main concerns. The different priorities of the two roles, while perfectly legitimate, can lead to situations of conflict. For example, as the change facilitator works to uncover people's concerns over changes and seeks to address these, there may be impacts on the project schedule and content that will be a major cause of frustration for the project manager. Such situations can be avoided or managed properly by the change facilitator. For example, by ensuring that the change facilitator and project manager are a unit working closely together and understanding each other's added value.

Lack of understanding of change facilitator's role

Another common experience with project managers is their lack of understanding or wrong assumptions made of change facilitators' role and scope. The idea here is not to generalize or criticize project managers. It is also your responsibility, as change facilitator, to correct any wrong assumptions, to make sure the project manager understands your role, where and how you will add value. This lack of understanding is a relatively common gap which exists in projects. It is essential to address this gap for a smooth transition.

An experience where this was blatant was a project where a company was opening a large customer service branch. The project manager was overseeing the refurbishment of the branch and the new integrated Customer Relationship Management system that would be launched first at this branch. The change facilitator was responsible for the smooth transition to the branch, both for staff adopting the new system and customers being aware of the new branch. In the brief meetings which the project manager and change facilitator had, the latter did not fully explain her role but jumped directly into the high level change management plan which included internal and external communication. The project manager asked a few questions on external communication, which the change facilitator described as communication to the customers that would feature the location of the new branch. The communication would also include the different services within the branch and the process from the customer walking in, getting a ticket number and completing a transaction.

The project manager thought this to mean that the change facilitator would handle all the physical signage to direct customers to the new branch as well as those inside the branch to indicate to customers which services were available. The change facilitator actually meant that existing customers would be emailed, website content would be updated, some brochures would be made and a new T.V. advert about the branch would be commissioned. You can imagine the chaos, panic and displeasure of all parties when one week before branch opening, at the meeting with the sponsor, everyone realized that no signage was available and no one wanted to take responsibility for it, arguing that it was not in their scope.

Mindset associated to the roles we play

Another common thing to hear on the ground among change facilitators is: "Project managers don't get what we do. They are too technical". You may feel that you have explained your role many times and the project managers still don't get it. Reign in your frustration and change tactics. Remember that you still need to get buy-in from project managers. You will want to make sure that they do not see you as being useless or as a threat. If they are unable to understand, you may need to speak in their language so keep in mind the approach that you need to have in explaining about change facilitation to different stakeholders. Explaining your role with concrete examples, where they see how your role complements theirs is useful. It is better to use IT examples if the project is IT infrastructure related. You can also explain what you will do by breaking it in different phases (in this case however, there may still be some grey areas regarding full understanding). Execute one phase and then link back to your explanation on your role and demonstrate the results of the action taken.

Planning for change

As a change facilitator you are aware that planning for the change
which is going to happen is essential. This is the only way to be able
to connect people to the particular change. The Change Adoption
Plan is the first step. As the LCtM[2] book highlights, a change
facilitator will need to undertake the following activities in order to
have a holistic Change Adoption Plan which is based on the
principles of the KDi's Adaptive Path Framework of Awareness-
Acceptance and Adoption:

- Change Analysis
- Stakeholder Analysis
- Impact Analysis
- Change Readiness Assessment
- Formulation of the Change Facilitation Strategy

A case study for conducting the Change and Impact Analysis will be
looked at here. It describes how the relationship model can give you
a helping hand at developing not just a robust Change Adoption Plan
but also one which can be executed with the desired result. An
important challenge faced by change facilitators is developing a plan
that can be endorsed and executed. The reality when working on a
change initiative is that you can be a great change facilitator with
excellent knowledge of your different change management
techniques and plans, but if the project manager(s) do not fully
collaborate and see you as a team member, you will struggle with the
change and impact analysis. As a result, you may end up with a diluted
analysis, an incomplete picture and an inadequate facilitation strategy.

---

[2] Dr. Nancy Harkrider and Tan Kim Leng (2013): Leading Change that Matters: Making Adoption a
Reality, 1st edition, KDI Asia Pte Ltd.

A change analysis consists of identifying what changes are going to happen and in which areas and the impact analysis then assesses the impacts of the change on the stakeholders. Both of these analyses are extremely important to the right strategy and resulting plan. The change analysis is quite challenging to undertake as you will quickly discover you need input from a combination of people to carry out this activity. Most people from the project implementation team will be able to talk endlessly about the new system being implemented and its benefits. However, to facilitate transition for end users and staff and understand their concerns and fears, you will need to be able to articulate the changes happening and not just the resulting benefits. A template of the change analysis table is provided below for a structured way of carrying out this activity. More resources and tools can be found in the LCtM book.

AREAS OF CHANGE	CHANGES	IMPLICATIONS	STAKEHOLDERS	
			Internal	External
Policy				
Operations				
Job Functions				
Technology				

Figure 5 - KDi Change Analysis

Case study of Choco Ltd:

Choco Ltd. is a medium sized company that produces chocolates. It has several key departments including manufacturing, sales, shipping accounting, human resources and IT.

The company decided to implement an Enterprise Resource Planning (ERP) software as it felt the existing systems had inefficiencies which an ERP system would be able to address. ERP is a business management software which a company can use to store and manage data from every stage of the business, including product planning, manufacturing, stock management, sales, shipping and payment. With an ERP system in place, Choco Ltd would have streamlined business processes and integrated information allowing it to improve operations and take the next steps towards growth.

Choco Ltd hired an ERP vendor for the implementation. The project management team consisted of a project manager from the ERP vendor and of a project manager internal to Choco Ltd. A change facilitator was also brought in to ensure a smooth transition as this change initiative was a big one with most of Choco Ltd.'s processes still being manual.

The change facilitator was introduced to the different team members as the person who would ensure a smooth transition. The vendor project manager felt that he was the one delivering the systems as well as the training and that his team would do the most important and challenging job. The company's internal project manager felt that his team was the one putting in the most effort to implement the new system and drive his people to adopt the changes. However none of these views were expressed and the change facilitator was welcomed and assured all parties would collaborate.

The first deliverable of the change facilitator was the Change Adoption Plan. In order to deliver this plan, one of the activities carried out by the change facilitator was the change and impact analysis. The stakeholder analysis had already been done by first understanding the organizational structure of Choco Ltd, talking to the project managers and department heads (middle management) and identifying Choco

Ltd.'s clients. In carrying out the change analysis, the facilitator sought to identify the areas of change as a result of the ERP implementation. Some common categories in which to group the changes are policy, operations, job functions and technology.

The change facilitator used various techniques to understand the changes which would be brought about. A lot of documentation such as project concept and project plans were provided to him. He also had meetings with the ERP vendor and Choco Ltd internal project manager. Both explained about the new system and its benefits but re-directed him to the project documents. Both did not appear convinced of the value the change facilitator would provide. Although the latter sensed this, he focused on getting his plan done and delved directly into the work. His priority was to concentrate on what needed to be done for the staff of Choco Ltd to be ready for the transition. He did not take the time to build a relationship with the project managers as, in his view, everyone was too busy and the deadlines were tight. His focus was on the staff undergoing the change. Relationship with the people implementing the change was a secondary thing.

The change facilitator managed to collate information mostly from documents provided to him and produce a change and impact analysis which guided the facilitation strategy in the Change Adoption Plan. The Change Adoption Plan was executed, along with the other deliverables such as the Change Communication Plan.

After new **system** *(ERP) deployment*

Many of Choco Ltd.'s staff experienced functions' change as they moved from manual processes to automated ones. Most changes were adopted as, in addition to technical training, staff had undergone change management training and communication had been carried out on the changes. However, one particular aspect, the invoicing function, did not work well.

During the project proposal and scope, direct invoicing by the ERP software was proposed as an optional item because Choco Ltd was not sure it wanted this tool. However during the implementation of the project, this option was exercised. It was indicated in an email that the project plan documents should be updated to reflect this but communication on this was mostly between the technical implementation teams. The version of documents consulted by the change facilitator did not include this and was therefore missed in the change and impact analysis as well as the Change Communication Plan.

Although staff received technical training on the new system, there were so many changes and new functions to learn that the new invoicing method, not covered in the communication plan, remained confusing and uncertain to end users.

The result was double invoicing to wholesalers. The system sent one invoice based on confirmation of delivery and the staff also manually sent an invoice as they were not aware that it was being done automatically. Some clients called to complain. Others with less sophisticated systems paid twice before realizing what was happening. This resulted in time and effort from Choco Ltd to understand what was happening. Staff thought it was a technical problem with the system as they were doing the invoicing as before and were certain it was correct. Accounting entries had to be reversed, attempts to salvage reputation and reassure clients were made and staff communication and training revisited.

How would the relationship model have enabled the change facilitator to have a more complete picture and therefore a more effective change adoption plan?

The relationship model promotes a one-team factor and in this case study, spending time to build the relationship would have enabled the change facilitator to see the views and territory fears of the project managers. A lot of information on pending changes are also in people's head rather than on paper. A project manager who understands the change facilitator role and sees how their two roles are complimentary is more likely to fill in the gaps with these pieces of missing information.

The challenging part in doing a change analysis is being able to capture what is going to change as opposed to how the new system would work. Most documentation available would cover the new proposed system and how it would work. To be able to understand "the change", the current way of operating needs to be understood as well. Some companies will have this documented in Standard Operating Procedures (SOPs) but very often, on the ground, the way people work deviates from the SOPs which have never been updated. In this case study, building the relationship with the internal project manager by gaining his trust would have allowed this manager to share more and the change facilitator would have been able to deliver a stronger change analysis.

Using this Knowledge to Strengthen Change Initiatives

The insights from the relationship approach can make a difference in change projects. Your role as change facilitator will intersect with that of the project manager at several points, the first being at the planning stage of your work. This is where you will need time from the project manager. Without buy-in from the project manager, it will be hard to get the needed information. In fact, it might be hard to get buy-in if the project manager is someone who is absorbed in the technical aspect and who has not worked with a change facilitator before or does not fully understand your role.

A positive relationship with project managers can make a difference in how they perceive your change facilitation role and your effectiveness in carrying out your mandate. But how do you build a strong relationship with project managers which ensures buy-in and cooperation? This is a key question that you need to ask yourself. Some strategies and tools for how to accomplish that are provided in the next paragraphs, but always remember to adapt these to the context in which you are working.

Before even attempting to build a relationship with the project managers, take a step back to understand their mindset. What are the typical concerns of a project manager and how can you, through change facilitation activities, help alleviate some of these concerns? The interaction that you will have with end users will be different from that of the project manager because your perspectives will be different. Therefore, you will likely gather valuable information through the Change Support Network which will help the project manager. This is your entry point to get buy-in from project managers as they will see that you are there to support them.

It may still be hard to have a fully collaborating project manager because the feedback on the ground that you are collecting from end users may not be something the project manager wants to hear since it may impact the project timeline, cost or scope. Knowing that this may be the case, right from the start of the project, be upfront about this aspect of your role. Make it clear that input from the ground will be available to the project manager and the project implementation plan needs to have some flexibility to take that into account.

Remind the project manager that a successful implementation is when the change is adopted, but unaddressed concerns from end users will not disappear. In fact, this is one of the reasons why many successfully implemented projects fail. Therefore you will want end users feedback to reach the project manager for it to be considered. However, input from the ground, coming to the project manager, left and right at points where irreversible decisions have been taken, will definitely not be helpful for the project. Nor will it help your relationship with the project manager. Some of this input from the ground might also be requests which have already been considered and not adopted for solid business reasons.

Therefore, in your early discussions with the project manager, be certain to review the interactions that have already happened with people on the ground. Often, end users who have their own idea of what needs to change may persist with the same requests. In addition, plan and agree on the category of inputs and most importantly, the different points in the project implementation schedule, where feedback will be taken from the ground. Categorization will give the project manager a sense of the type of issues which may arise and the planned timing will help integrate input into the project as well as handle dependencies.

Keeping in mind how challenging the relationship with the project manager can be but also how essential it is to have a positive relationship, put into practice some techniques of change facilitation to build your relationship with project managers. As you would with the end users, identify the resistance points of the project manager and address them. Ensure the project manager is aware of your role by sharing about change facilitation and its contribution to the success of a project. Work toward the project manager's acceptance of the change facilitation team by demonstrating your added value.

Finally become an aligned team as the project manager adopts your plan and approach. With this approach, you will build a relationship with the project manager so that the Change Facilitator-Project Manager roles become complimentary and create win-win situations. A smooth transition is, after all, the responsibility of an aligned team.

Strategies and Tools

You will want to build a positive working relationship which is secure enough to discuss and resolve differences and which makes a team stronger. A strategy to start with is to clearly define roles and responsibilities. Defining these roles and responsibilities for each team is simple but it will help tremendously in setting the scene, having a clear picture and avoiding misunderstandings on scope. It is unfortunately often overlooked or conducted at a very high level, where only the job titles are provided. As a result, different teams working together do not necessarily grasp the value-add or challenges faced by other teams.

In defining the roles and responsibilities, it is recommended that the change facilitator, team lead and the project manager meet first. This gives an excellent opportunity for these team leaders to get to know each other and set the scene for their collaboration. The broader project team and change facilitation team should join in this exercise once the managers have met. They are, after all, the people who will interact at the working level and will need to understand each other's roles.

Once roles are defined, they should not just be written down in a document, which in all likelihood no one will actually have time to look at. Instead it should be communicated to all the core internal stakeholders involved or impacted by the project. Such communication will reinforce the "one team" feel and will also pave the way for interaction with your impacted stakeholders. This exercise will enable the envisioning of how objectives of the two teams fit together to achieve the goals of the project being undertaken.

Once you have taken that first step towards a positive relationship by defining and communicating roles and responsibilities, you can further build teams' relationship through the following:

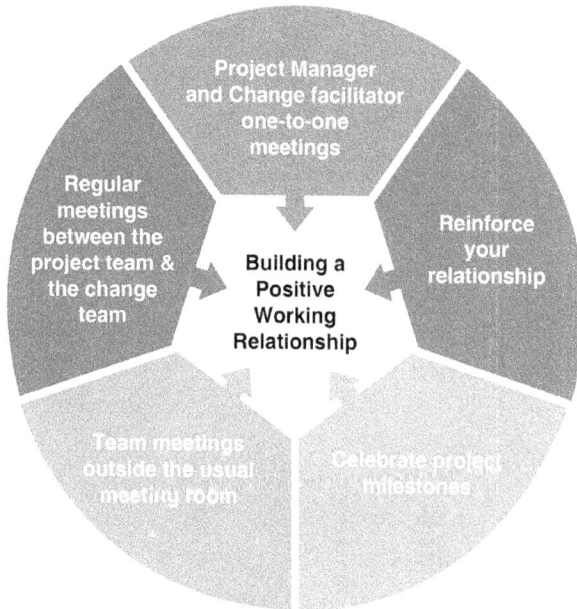

Figure 6 – Building a Positive Working Relationship

- Hold regular meetings between the project team and the change team.

In addition to being a venue for updates and concerns, this is where your teams will see where their work intersects and where they can help each other. Often if a project is experiencing issues, it is felt at the implementation level as delays and at the change level as resistance.

- The project manager and the change facilitator team lead should also have one-to-one meetings

As you build a stronger relationship of trust and respect with each other, it becomes easier to discuss and resolve differences. Lead by example and you will find your respective team members working better together.

- Reinforce your relationship: never take it for granted

Starting with a good work relationship does not mean that it will last. You have to keep building the relationship, acknowledging that a positive work relationship contributes to successful project implementation.

- Organize certain team meetings outside the usual meeting room

Your environment affects your behavior. You will find that when you meet in the same meeting room, people will often take the same seats and position. If you change the environment and conduct a meeting over a nice lunch you might find that both teams relax and approach issues differently.

- Celebrate project milestones

All key stakeholders driving project implementation need a moment of pause to recognize what has been achieved. A simple celebration when completing project milestones will go a long way to maintaining enthusiasm and momentum. It will also contribute to team cohesiveness.

"There is nothing more difficult to take in hand, more perilous to conduct, or more uncertain in its success, than to take the lead in the introduction of a new order of things."

Niccolo Machiavelli

CHAPTER 5

Beyond Reporting

The Change Facilitator and the Sponsor

Overview

Reporting is a key activity in all projects. There are various approaches and styles: some industry specific, others adopting the latest methods or finding more innovative means to report progress updates to the sponsor (upper management, responsible to oversee the project). While there is no question that reporting remains a must, the relationship model puts forward the need to go beyond reporting and to build a relationship of trust with the sponsor, something that can be otherwise neglected.

Your role as change facilitator will be to map a change path which staff will embark upon enthusiastically and as a united team. This change map will need to be done strategically after readiness assessments and staff engagements. However, even a strong change management plan will not produce the intended results if it is not endorsed and supported by top management.

On change facilitators' role in mapping the path to people-centric change, Tan Kim Leng asserted, "This is the Change Facilitator's most elemental contribution to project success. Once the plan is completed and endorsed by the upper management, the Change Facilitator's role is legitimized."

A relationship of trust is an asset that will help you as change facilitators in navigating, from the project manager and middle management, to the sponsor. You will be able to leverage the sponsor's influence and power to get much needed time with project managers and middle management. You can then link back to the sponsor with important feedback from end users and teams on the ground. This chapter provides a high level view of the different categories in which sponsors fall and how best to build your credibility and trust with them while avoiding pitfalls. It looks at some challenges that you will face in one form or another with sponsors and proposes a series of strategies to build trust.

The Change Facilitator and the Sponsor

It is obvious that you will put the sponsor as a high priority when you make your key stakeholders list. In fact you will want them to be satisfied and pleased with your work and you will make sure to report progress. But the key question to ask yourself is how to move from a simple reporting relationship to one where you are able to add value to the sponsor's vision of the change initiative and to ensure that the latter is engaged in generating a positive buzz for the project.

According to the KPMG New Zealand Project Management Survey 2010, a common reason for project failures is a lack of executive sponsorship and management buy-in. As a change facilitator, you will need to guide and convince the sponsor to embrace and lead the change and, to do that, it is essential to have the sponsor's trust. As you connect with the sponsor and the other two key stakeholders – the project manager and middle management, you will be able to identify gaps and problem areas in their relationships with each other.

For example, a project where a sponsor micro-manages the project manager will face bottlenecks in decision-making that causes delays.

Different types of sponsors

Sponsors will be different based on their personality, length of time in their current role, the type of organization they work in and the change initiative itself. Some sponsors are very strong leaders, have a clear vision of the project's goals and have considerable influence over their staff. Other sponsors can be somewhat new in their position and have less buy-in from their people.

There are also cases where sponsors are handed a project they don't really believe in from higher hierarchy management, but which they have to execute. Politically minded sponsors are yet another category. Whether it is corporate politics or political aspirations for example in the case of public sector reform projects, it can be a landmine to navigate. Another challenging situation is when you have a group of sponsors overseeing the project. Ultimately, there will be one chairperson and decision maker but you will most likely need more time to observe and assess their influences, pressure points and dynamics. You will need to be very careful not to be caught in the politics in such cases.

Sponsors may not fall in one specific category but are likely be a mix of the above examples. One important skill for a change facilitator to develop and refine is the ability to read and assess people. This will help in knowing the approach to take to build trust. Moreover, depending on the type of sponsor they are, their concerns and pressure points will vary. Identifying the main concerns of the sponsor and proposing strategies to address them will go a long way in gaining the trust of sponsors.

However, the tricky part is identifying the real concerns of sponsors. Bear in mind that sponsors' biggest worry may not be something that they will communicate to you as it may not be directly linked to the change initiative. For example, the next big step in the sponsor's career may be riding on how well they execute a particular change initiative.

A possible caveat

Does the sponsor understand what change facilitation is? Just because you have been given a role in a change initiative does not mean that the sponsor fully understands change facilitation. Some projects funded by big donor organizations may require a change management component, others may have a change component integrated with the Program Management Office which the client signed up for. Therefore, it is important to establish the level of understanding of your sponsor about change facilitation and to manage sponsors' expectations as they may have made wrong assumptions about the scope. The difficulty in managing this aspect is that you will have to be careful not to appear disrespectful to the sponsor.

From interactions to relationship building

The opportunity here, however, is to build your relationship with the sponsor by making time to clarify your role and scope. For a relationship to be built at this stage, it needs to go beyond going through your contract and deliverables. Moreover, if your sponsors are unfamiliar with change facilitation, just going through the scope may not help in guiding their understanding. People understand much more through a story where they can visualize and retain key messages. The strategy is to share your past experiences on change facilitation. Highlight the successes while being upfront about the challenges you met with. This is not something you might expect to have to do after winning the contract or being assigned the role (if you are an in-house change facilitator) but keep in mind that while you have walked through the door, you are yet to gain the trust of the sponsor.

Case Study of Better Life Insurance Ltd:

Better Life Insurance Ltd is a decade year old company providing insurance services such as health and life insurance. It has so far provided only traditional insurance products. It is well established in the industry but latest surveys showed that market perceived Better Life Insurance Ltd to be old-style as well as not dynamic and innovative enough. As a result, and in response to a changing and more competitive market, Better Life Ltd decided to offer a greater range of insurance products with more complex financing. It held strategic sessions to formulate the new vision of the company, its positioning and the next ten years growth plan.

Better Life Ltd's new vision was to become an innovative, highly agile organization. It realized that change agility is something which must be built into the organization's foundation. Therefore to have a truly adaptable work force, Better Life Ltd decided that it would continuously implement projects. The idea was that this would make them highly proactive, enabling them not to miss interesting opportunities and reinforcing their brand name.

First, however, an IT modernization project was needed to have the right infrastructure in place. Following that, Better Life Ltd would proceed with other changes. It was decided that changes would keep flowing in the form of latest updates to work system and other innovative projects. The strategy to become change agile was to have change projects follow each other non-stop.

The IT Modernization project

The needed governance structure for the IT modernization project was put in place with a sponsor overseeing the project, middle management involved and an internal project manager working with a project manager from the IT vendor company. A change facilitator consultant was brought on board. A project implementation plan, focusing only on the IT modernization project was designed and agreed upon.

The change facilitator's key deliverables consisted of the change facilitation strategy and plan as well as a change manual, intended for Better Life Ltd staff to be able to plan change communications in the future. The sponsor briefed the change facilitator only on the IT modernization project, briefly including the vision of Better Life Ltd wanting to become innovative and change agile but did not mention the continuous projects which would follow the IT modernization project. The change facilitator found the sponsor to be distant and very reserved when providing the overall vision of the project.

However, at the same time, the change facilitator saw that the sponsor was a strong leader and was very supportive especially when it came to endorsing the change plan and ensuring middle management's collaboration to have a Change Support Network. With the sponsor fulfilling his role within the change plan – communicating and engaging with staff on the IT modernization project, the change facilitator did not spend time building her relationship with the sponsor.

Transition to the new IT system went well. Staff understood the changes and benefits of the new system. The adoption phase also went well with training provided more holistic - focusing on role and function changes in addition to training on the new system.

The change manual was the last deliverable and was submitted at the end of the change facilitator's contract. This coincided with the time of new system launch and core staff was busy and focused on final fine tuning needed and training and the change manual found its way to the bottom pile of documents to go through. At the closing meeting, the change facilitator highlighted to the sponsor the need to have trained change agents in addition to the change manual. The change facilitator was surprised to see the sponsor looking displeased and did not understand the negative response.

The IT modernization project having been completed, the change facilitator left the company with the satisfaction of a job well done.

Becoming a change agile organization with new changes flowing in non-stop through new projects

Shortly after the IT infrastructure was modernized, Better Life Ltd started implementing new projects, some taking the form of updates to the new system and others being projects, taking 3-6 months to implement. As these changes kicked in, problems within the organization started. Staff were confused and uncertain of the reasons of these changes. The updates to the system required staff to acknowledge the email, install the updates and read a manual attached in the email. Some rumors about the IT modernization project not having been done successfully started. People did not understand why these updates were needed when a new system had just been implemented. As other projects started, and staff found some of their job functions changing again, they resisted. While they had understood the need to modernize and had adopted new practices and job functions, they were reluctant to again change roles. Additional rumors on the stability of the company started and staff began worrying about their jobs. Some even began looking for another job.

Communication about the new changes were done by a small group from the core implementation team using the recommendations and templates in the change manual but it did not suffice as people did not understand why these changes were happening.

Where did it all go wrong?

The awareness phase of the change facilitation plan focused only on the IT modernization project, its benefits and changes. It did not cover changes to come and the positioning that the organization was after. Instead of the IT modernization project being the means to achieve the necessary foundation to move towards a change agile organization, the IT modernization project became the end goal. The objectives communicated to staff on the modernization project did include Better Life Ltd becoming innovative and change agile. However, staff were not able to link that objective to the flow of non-stop changes happening after the IT modernization project.

Since the change facilitator did not know about the overall vision, she did not set the IT modernization project within this context. Later , when the team from the core staff used the change manual, they only communicated about the changes, instead of facilitating the change.

Facilitating change involves explaining what the changes are, its reasons, assessing their impact and engaging with those impacted, all while using communication as a tool.

Why did the sponsor withhold the full vision of the company that included a series of projects to increase change agility?

The IT modernization project was expensive and the follow up projects would also be costly. The sponsor knew there was budget only to hire the change facilitator for the first project. Having had some bad experiences previously with suppliers and being of a suspicious nature, the sponsor was afraid that the change facilitator would hold back on the change manual or would make sure to get an extension if the latter knew of the upcoming projects.

While the sponsor understood the basics of change management, he did not really understand how change facilitators work and why the overall vision was so crucial.

Could a relationship of trust help in this situation?

It is clear that the sponsor felt he could not talk about the follow up changes, which would happen directly after the infrastructure project. The change facilitator sensed some wariness on the sponsor's part but because she had the needed support to execute the facilitation strategy she did not make time to build a trusting relationship with the sponsor.

Had she gained the trust of the sponsor, the change facilitator could have focused the awareness and acceptance phase on the notion of change facility – the bigger picture of where the organization is heading and why there would be many more projects to come.

It is true that it would have taken time to build a relationship of trust with the sponsor. In fact, it is likely that by the time the sponsor would have embraced the full vision, the awareness phase would have been well underway. However, the change facilitator could still have re-designed the acceptance phase or could have formulated another facilitation strategy to ensure staff would expect continuous change. The right strategy would have encouraged enthusiasm for the continuous change, engaging staff in the change and reassuring them so that they do not fear the impact on their work.

Using this Knowledge to Strengthen Change Initiatives

The knowledge that you will encounter different types of sponsors with different motivations and that you have to steadily engage with them to build a relationship of trust can make you more aware in your interactions with them. Valuable input during the initial analysis of a project at the "planning for change" stage will come from the sponsor. Whatever the change initiative, it stems from the sponsor's vision and a big picture perspective of where an organization wants to be.

This bigger picture is an important aspect for a change facilitator to flesh out and understand as this will be the soul of the change initiative. This bigger picture will bring meaning to staff when communicating the project. While project managers will be able to articulate the details of the project from beginning to end, it is the sponsor who will be able to provide the strategic direction of the project, thus reinforcing your change facilitation plans.

An engaged sponsor can also help open doors for change facilitators. One common element across most projects is how busy everyone is, from the project management team to the end users.

As a change facilitator, you will need time with different groups of people to understand the changes resulting from the project. Similarly, when carrying out change readiness assessment, staff will need to take time to answer survey questions or attend focus groups. Having a sponsor who understands and supports the change facilitator will make a big difference. For example, staff is more likely to be responsive to the change facilitator because they have received a memo from the sponsor.

The relationship approach can also help strengthen the change facilitator's plans for the awareness phase. Communication about the change initiative is important and during the awareness phase, the project details are shared with the staff. Some project messages may need to be delivered by the sponsor, who is a leader staff trust and look up to. During the acceptance and adoption phase as well, the sponsor may be called upon to motivate staff.

The sponsor will also be keen to get the pulse from the ground up and information from the Change Support Network can be fed back to the sponsor. Often, the sponsor does not have time or access to talk to end users. The change facilitator can act as a connection point in being a communication bridge both from sponsor to end users and from end users to sponsors. Indeed a change facilitator who is able to connect sponsors and end users by navigating across these different relationships, with proposed solutions to carefully evaluated issues, will be better able to work towards a smooth transition.

Strategies and Tools: Building trust with the sponsor

The relationship approach puts forward the need to build trust with the sponsor so as to be able to play the role of key connection point. Building trust takes time and on a project, it may often seem that there will not be enough time to do this. Some may compare building trust to brick building which takes time, effort, patience and is done one brick at a time. However, as a change facilitator, it is crucial that you plan for this trust building time because, down the line, it will make a big difference. This is the case when it comes to the execution of your change facilitation plan or when faced with obstacles.

How does one build trust? You have to be strategic about it. First, be fully aware of your objective for building trust with the sponsor. With that thought in mind, weave in actions which will help towards trust in every interaction you have with the sponsor. Earlier on, the notion that sponsors differ from one another and that you will have to be skillful at reading and assessing them was raised. Your assessment of the sponsor will guide you in developing a strategic approach to build trust. General techniques exist and these are covered below but the most important tip is to develop an approach customized to your sponsor and the context in which you are operating. This can be built from the general techniques but adapted to your particular sponsor. As your interactions with the sponsor grow, refine your observations and assessments and modify your trust building strategy accordingly.

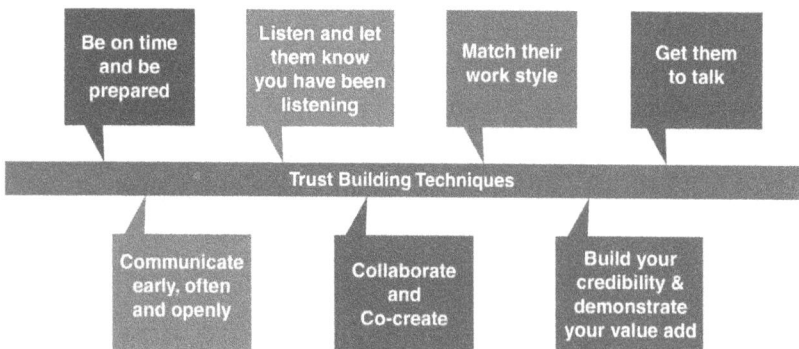

Figure 7 – Trust Building Techniques

- Sponsors are usually busy people, so make sure to respect their time and be extremely well prepared for the meetings that you have with them.

Being well prepared means not only being ready with your presentation/report but also having thought ahead of the concerns that the sponsor may have and being ready with some proposed responses. Also be ready with a trust building action for every meeting.

- Listen and ensure the sponsor knows you have been listening.

Use techniques of active listening such as paraphrasing, clarifying and summarizing. Non-verbal signs such as eye contact, the active listener's posture and mirroring can also help demonstrate you are listening.

- Match their work style.

You will best be able to communicate with them if you do so in their style. This means saying things in a way so that they can actually hear it and not simply saying it how you feel it. Speaking the same "language" is key. Everyone operates in different frames and you need to get into their frame to deliver your key messages.

Try to also match their conversation pace. If they speak slowly and your usual style is to speak really fast, slow down in a natural way to match them.

You can also find out their preference in communication medium for day to day interactions. Although remember that nothing beats face-to-face time.

- Get them to talk

Get sponsors to talk about the long term vision and strategy. This is useful for a number of reasons. It will enable you to get the context and overall objective of the project, which you need when planning and implementing change. Employees are better able to contribute to innovation and growth of the organization when they have the big picture view. Beyond that, getting a sponsor to talk will bring you closer to the latter as you will get a better understanding of their interests and priorities. Ensure that the sponsor elaborates on the long term plan by asking guiding questions.

Try to elevate the discussion and even move to other projects led by the sponsors. First get them to tell you about the successful projects and why they were a success but then get them to also talk about challenges they regularly experience in implementing projects. Once a sponsor is talking to you about obstacles experienced with past project or projects which have failed, you will know that you are moving in a good direction in the trust scale.

- Communicate early, often and openly.

Engaging early on with the sponsor is extremely important. One of your first interactions with the sponsor should be about your role, responsibilities, deliverables and intended outcomes so that the sponsor knows what to expect. If your sponsor is not well versed in change facilitation, this strategy will address that. It will also help in cases where the sponsor is not too involved in the project.

Communicating often does not mean just sending a weekly report. You cannot assume that all your reports and progress updates will be read. Where organizations have a formal weekly status report, make sure to know what the sponsor looks for in the short executive summary. If an organization does not have an established method, then you will want to recommend and help create one.

Moreover, you will need to find a way to be visible and to have major issues and progress be reported to upper management. A technique is to clarify what level of issue needs to be elevated to and addressed by the sponsor. Many project issues should be addressed by the working groups and do not need to be elevated to the sponsor unless they will result in missing a milestone. When you are establishing the work process, try your best to emphasize the need for regular but short meetings for this type of updates. Be open and honest about the situation. Sponsors hate to be surprised.

- Collaborate and Co-Create – don't just stick to your strategy and plan.

Some of your proposed strategy might not work in the sponsor's organization or country. By collaborating with the sponsor, you are enabling the project leaders to co-create a solution that will work. The result will be a more implementable change facilitation plan and the sponsor's buy-in. Make sure to give the sponsor credit.

The difficulty comes in cases where you strongly feel that the sponsor's ideas will not contribute to the objective of having staff accept and adopt the change initiative. If even after diplomatically sharing your views, the sponsor persistently brings up their idea, you will need to re-evaluate. Sponsors may have motivations and agendas beyond the project and you may need to compromise to some extent so as not to lose their support.

- Build your credibility and demonstrate your value add early on.

Informally share some of your experience of working on change initiatives – the challenges faced and how they were overcome. Remember that it is not a pitch session. It needs to be more subtle. Find a way to slip it in the conversation as an example to demonstrate something. Showing your value add early on also helps as it will quickly lead to the sponsor being reassured of your abilities.

Delivering solutions to the sponsor is another useful technique. When you identify an issue, which the sponsor needs to be made aware of or take action on, include impacts and possible solutions with the presentation of the problem. Moreover, if the organization is new to change facilitation, make sure to show your value by addressing or alleviating a particular concern quite fast. It doesn't have to be something big but delivering on the small things will enhance your credibility and make the sponsor trust that you will deliver on the big things.

"Keeping people at the center of your change initiatives is the only path for increasing your chances of success."

Tan Kim Leng

CHAPTER 6

Engage People in the Change

The Change Facilitator and Middle Management

Overview

A change facilitator ensures that projects being implemented are people centered. Focusing on people means involving and engaging with them. Who are the people who need to be engaged? In planning for change you will carry out your stakeholder analysis as well as your change and impact analysis. Your interaction and engagement with stakeholders will vary according to their role in the project and how the project impacts them. To better understand how people in organizations will see and subsequently react to change, you will need to understand their perspectives. The LCtM[3] book explores the lenses through which different layers of the organization see their world. Organizational leaders, the ones at the upper management level have

---

[3] Dr. Nancy Harkrider and Tan Kim Leng (2013): Leading Change that Matters: Making Adoption a Reality, 1st edition, KDI Asia Pte Ltd.

a strategic view. Middle managers supervise and see the situation while employees' view is based on their needs and limitations. Faced with change, employees will have one question in mind, "How does this affect me?"

Organizational Leaders	Middle Managers	Staff
Telescopic View	Macroscopic View	Microscopic View
See the future	See the situation	See the details

Figure 8 – KDi Organizational Perspectives

In talking about people centered change, it is the people most impacted by the change who are being referenced and to whom you must reach out. Usually the frontline or operations staff or end users of system are the ones most impacted by the change happening. For example, when a growing textile company decided to change its quality management system, the staff on the assembly line are the ones who will be most impacted by this change. Communication on the change will need to be done well in advance of the launch of a new quality management system. Employees will have to not only be trained on the new processes but also engaged to see the benefits of new system so that they accept the change and then adopt the new processes. As a change facilitator in such a project, the target audience of your change implementation plan (e.g. readiness assessments, communication plans) will be these employees.

How do you access these employees? Most of time, it is impossible for the change facilitator to talk to every staff person. Some forms of communication such as Frequently Asked Questions (FAQs) and websites are valuable in allowing you to push information to staff but will not bring you feedback and questions. Forming a Change Support Network (CSN) is one way to get staff representation from each department. You can then leverage on this network to get the feedback from staff. Doing roadshows is another way you can communicate with staff while at the same time engaging them. However, these modes of communication and engagement rely heavily on willingness of staff to participate.

The key message here is that when you are at the planning stage for change, you need to reflect about how best to access and ensure participation of the people who are at the center of the change initiative. You cannot assume easy access to staff and must consider who are the gate keepers to the people. In this chapter, middle management is positioned as a key stakeholder group, who can give you access to staff. Therefore, a strong working relationship with middle management is crucial to be able to work towards a smooth transition.

Middle managers, often called the backbone of organizations, usually focus on developing specific plans to reach the organizational objectives set by top management. Depending on the organization's hierarchy, the middle management is usually responsible for two lower levels of junior staff. Middle managers are often referred to as department head or manager. They will be the ones operating up and down the chain of command, as the conduit between the executive level and the front line. This chapter looks at the implications of middle management being gate keepers to staff. It also puts forward the concerns and change issues of middle management. Focusing on navigation skills, which the middle manager and change facilitator are likely to have in common, is proposed to build relationships. Navigation skills here refer to the set of diplomatic, influencing and emotional intelligence skills, which both middle managers and change facilitators need to have, given the nature of their roles.

The change facilitator and middle management

Like sponsors, middle managers will definitely be included in the stakeholder analysis that you will carry out as part of planning for change. However, middle managers are often overlooked in terms of the relationship aspect. This is because we often assume that the sponsor and middle management will be well aligned on the change initiative. We often put all of management in one basket and assume that the sponsor driving the project has the buy-in of the management committee. We assume that if the sponsor is happy, the middle management will also be happy.

Middle managers – gate keepers to the Change Support Network

However, in most project experiences, the reality is different. Middle managers sandwiched between top management and staff have a different outlook on organizational change compared to sponsors or staff. Middle management have an in-depth understanding of the details of the business processes which sponsors and upper management often lack. As a result, middle management will have concerns and even resistance factors, which will need to be addressed. If concerns and input of middle management are not carefully analyzed and worked through, new systems and processes will likely fail.

Middle management are also the ones who can grant access to end users and employees. Therefore a strong rapport with middle managers is essential so that the strategy of having a Change Support

Network(CSN) can have a chance of achieving the objectives of its creation. Having a CSN is highly recommended as part of the change facilitation strategy. It is an invaluable source of information and support in helping you in your change facilitation role. However, without middle managers' support, it will fail. Middle managers usually have the trust of the end users/staff and are the gatekeepers, thus controlling access to the people most highly impacted by change in an organization.

Therefore middle managers represent another key stakeholder group with whom it is crucial for you to have a strong relationship in order to be able to facilitate change in an organization. While the sponsor will have the vision of the change initiative and see the future of an organization and staff will see the details relating to the changes impacting them, the middle managers are the ones who see the situation that needs to be managed. Operating up and down the chain of command, they have the difficult task of navigating between two essential groups of stakeholders belonging inside the organization. Such navigation skills are something which change facilitators will have in common with middle managers and this can serve as the bridge for relationship building.

However, you need to keep in mind that there are also situations where this bridge does not exist because some middle managers you will encounter will not have these skills. They either fight with upper management all the time or tell their work groups and front line employees that the change is being forced on them and there is nothing they can do. Such cases will make it more difficult and will call upon your own navigation skills even more. You can still build a rapport in such cases and, if middle managers are receptive, you may even find yourself coaching them in an informal manner or recommending the sponsor to strengthen the mid-level capability.

Middle managers' shifts in positioning

Change projects are often synonymous to stressful times for middle
managers. Responsible for connecting top management's vision to
staff and for helping staff during transition time, middle managers
themselves need to accept and adapt to change. In addition, they need
to ensure that business is running as smoothly as possible during
transition times. There is a high risk that middle managers find
themselves burning out during implementation of change initiatives.
Unfortunately, this is often linked to a lack of readiness for change.
Even if, at the start of a project, middle managers are open to the
change, they may start to resist and oppose changes as the intensity
of work and difficulties linked to transition time increases. When
work gets done more slowly right after implementation or as the new
processes require fine tuning, middle managers may get more stressed
and may want to revert to old systems and processes As a change
facilitator if you have not built a strong relationship with middle
managers and do not continuously engage with them, you may find
yourself caught by surprise as the latter start changing their position
to oppose the project.

Concerns of middle managers and change issues

Key concerns of middle managers will be on the quality of training
provided on new processes and systems and on how changes affect
staff performance. Intricately linked within these concerns are
"people issues" which as a change facilitator you can help ease.
However, without significant engagement with middle managers, the
latter may be unable to articulate these difficulties as change
problems, leaving them to be addressed by the project
manager/vendor whose technical perspective may not suffice in
addressing people challenges. A relationship with middle managers

will ensure that they understand how they can leverage on your change facilitation skills to have a smooth transition. Otherwise, many change issues will be missed or left unaddressed. Other challenges highlighted in earlier chapters about stakeholders' lack of understanding on the change facilitation role are also relevant here.

Assessing change readiness

During the planning for change stage, you will need to carry out a change readiness assessment to get a sense of the preparedness (willingness and mindset) of employees for change as well as their capability for change. This will provide a channel for the operational, emotive and assumptive concerns[4] of employees to be expressed. While it makes sense for the first change readiness exercise to be done well before project scope finalization and kick off, in reality, this rarely happens. Instead the change facilitation component is activated too late after major decisions have been made, giving less time to prepare for the change.

So where does that leave you? As you will carry out the change readiness assessment, the project manager's team and vendor will be finalizing technical requirements and establishing a go-live date. The sequencing of activities relating to the "planning for change" stage is rarely in the timeframe that you wish it to be within the overall project plan. You will be running to get your change and impact analysis and readiness assessment done to be able to define your facilitation strategy and execute your action plan.

What can really help you at that point, where you come in "too late" in the project, is the relationship with the stakeholders. A strong

---

[4] Dr. Nancy Harkrider and Tan Kim Leng (2013): Leading Change that Matters: Making Adoption a Reality, 1st edition, KDI Asia Pte Ltd.

rapport of trust will make all the difference. If you start off building a good relationship with middle managers, you will be able to formalize a CSN faster and tap into that resource right away for the change readiness assessment. In some cases, there might also be ways to get the change readiness questions inserted into the project manager's assessment process. It does mean that you would have to be on board early enough for this to happen. Usually this can work well with in-house project managers and change facilitators. It is more challenging with external consultants.

Change readiness assessments are usually done through confidential surveys. An important limitation to be aware of is that in certain cultures the confidentiality nature of the assessment will not reassure employees to provide their honest opinions. Therefore, it will be important to structure and phrase questions in a reassuring and, at times indirect way. A good relationship with middle management can guide you to know about employees' perceptions. Moreover, this is where your CSN can add value by testing your readiness assessment and also by validating your findings. In other cultures, having the assessment be public and attributable to individual respondents might bring a sense of ownership.

This really depends on the country and organizational culture.

Case Study of Meyer Prix:

Meyer Prix, a hypermarket (mega store) operating in a developing country for over 10 years decided to introduce a loyalty card points program to its customers.

The project of introducing loyalty cards was a big one as Meyer Prix had a huge base of regular customers. Top management's (CEO and board of directors) vision was for Meyer Prix to be positioned as an innovative and leading hypermarket being the first one in the country to be introducing fidelity cards. Another part of their vision was to start building their database of customer shopping patterns through the loyalty card to be able to work with brands that provide customers with offers and promotions. The loyalty card, together with data collected would also enable them to offer customers personalized vouchers.

The project manager was from the IT department and was responsible for delivering a relational database for loyalty cards. He was overseen closely by his department head. The heads of various departments including the marketing department, operations department and customer service department were also involved in the project. Meyer Prix's objective was to issue at least 100,000 cards in the first month of the card launch. This was an ambitious target but it was linked to Meyer Prix's marketing strategy and vision of building its database to be able to work with product brands.

A change facilitator was brought in to work on this change initiative to ensure that staff adopted the change and new practices and also to support the external communication.

The governance of this change project was headed by a steering committee, chaired by the CEO. Members of the steering committee were the heads of departments as well as some selected managers and team leaders. The change facilitator engaged with the CEO (sponsor) and the project manager right from the start, building a good relationship and ensuring they understood the value add of change facilitation. The notion of having a Change Support Network (CSN) was proposed by the change facilitator and approved by the sponsor and the steering committee.

The idea was for the CSN to be formed with representatives from each department. Departments were slow to send the names of staff who would form part of that network. Precious time was spent in following up on the set-up of the network and the first CSN meeting had to be rescheduled a few times. Meanwhile the change readiness assessment was being prepared to get a feel of the willingness and capability for change of Meyer Prix. The change facilitator consulted with the project manager to understand the different impacts of upcoming changes on Meyer Prix and accordingly prepare the readiness assessment. The facilitator also wanted to consult with the CSN to vet the assessment but as the latter was still in process of being formed and with time running out, the change readiness assessment had to be launched.

The change readiness assessment was carried out after the project scope was approved. The change facilitator knew that, while the assessment would give a rough feel of the situation, the results would be skewed towards higher level of confidence in the change as staff would be careful in sharing their views since they would not want to appear against the project. Acknowledging that this is a common limitation of change readiness assessment, the change facilitator was counting on face-to-face meetings with the CSN to dig deeper and uncover the more subjective, emotional and assumptive concerns as well as resistance factors. The first meeting with the CSN finally took place and the members of the network validated the results of the readiness assessment, which showed staff as having a high level of confidence and high preparedness for change and high capability for change. The change facilitator managed to identify some concerns especially from the customer care staff who felt they did not have enough information on the loyalty program due to lack of communication between the customer care and marketing department.

This first CSN meeting was somewhat satisfactory, although the change facilitator hoped that CSN members would be more participative at future meetings. It was not uncommon for a CSN to start slowly and therefore the change facilitator was not too worried. However, during later stages of change planning and implementation, the change facilitator found it difficult to tap into the CSN. Some CSN members excused themselves due to work load and being busy in other work groups for the project while others did not reply or attend. The change facilitator raised the issue to the sponsor who directed the heads of department to provide their support. However, further convocation of the CSN still did not result in its members showing up. Having to stick to the timeline, the change facilitator had to start implementing the change strategy and internal communication plan, without the CSN's support.

Some results of not having a functioning CSN

- The change facilitator did not have "eyes and ears" on the ground and struggled to identify some of the deep-rooted concerns.

- The proposed change facilitation strategy was not co-created with the people of the organization and resulted in lack of ownership of staff as well as execution challenges.

- The staff did not become ambassadors for the change.

- The change facilitator was unable to catch rumors and negativity evolving around the project.

One issue with very high impact, which was not picked up by the change facilitator, was negative rumors among staff, especially cashiers and customer care staff. These rumors were caused by the bad experience of significant system downtime and angry customers to deal with, the last time that Meyer Prix went through an IT change. Cashiers and customer care agents were worried about dealing with long queues and angry clients. As a result, they did not embrace the marketing campaign, launched a few months before the loyalty card was out, which leveraged on employees, mentioning the loyalty card and giving out flyers

The staff concern was an assumptive and emotional one that could have been addressed easily. The previous IT change was a centralization of the till system and downtime did mean long queues with customers being unable to pay. The loyalty card program was less risky as the contingency would be for the customer to keep the receipt for their points to be updated if ever the loyalty card system was down. However, rumors left to fester created a wave of non-enthusiastic staff.

Why did the CSN fail, in spite of the idea being validated by the steering committee?

It is important to observe and understand a steering committee's dynamics. Discussions usually stay at a high level and direction and approvals are obtained from a steering committee. Making things happen on the ground after the approval of a steering committee, however, does not automatically follow. There is a need to engage with people even, if in principle, they agreed to the idea. In Meyer Prix's situation, there was no targeted engagement with heads of department beyond the steering committee. The change facilitator assumed that with the sponsor supporting the idea of having a CSN, everyone would fall in line. However, this did not happen for several reasons.

The head of operations of Meyer Prix did not see the benefit of a loyalty card program. He was not convinced it could help with brands promotions. For him, it was a marketing strategy and it did not interest him. He was involved in a negotiation with an important wholesaler to offer a new product and that was taking a lot of his time. He had delegated a team to handle product labeling and shelves for the loyalty card points. He saw it as a time consuming activity for his team and could not see the point of delegating more staff to the CSN. As he was responsible for business to continue as usual during the implementation, he was against releasing any cashiers for them to attend CSN meetings.

The marketing manager was focused on the external communication campaign. His team was already working overtime and he did not encourage anyone to join the CSN. The head of customer care was upset that the marketing department was not sharing enough detailed information on how the card would work. He felt that his people would be the ones facing customers and should have been part of the core team. Some of these concerns were raised in the first CSN meeting but when subsequent CSN meetings did not happen, the head of customer care found the CSN as an ineffective platform.

How could the relationship model have helped?

- A way for the change facilitator to address pressure points and gain support

The relationship model is based on the three key stakeholders groups who need to build a strong relationship. This in turn becomes a form of support and a means of making things move forward, an essential element in change projects.

Engaging with the head of operations would have allowed the change facilitator to detect his lack of interest. In facilitating change, it is crucial to detect groups who will not embrace the change, not because they are against it but because they do not feel it matters. Such groups can cause a lot of inertia and be the bottleneck during implementation.

Building a relationship with the head of marketing would have helped the change facilitator to bridge the gap between marketing and customer care. The marketing department in focusing solely on external communication was losing the impact of having internal staff as card ambassadors.

- Access to people impacted by the change

A relationship with the head of customer care would have ensured the latter's continuous feedback. Some CSN do not work in the formal and structured manner planned but still manage to serve their purpose in a more informal way. In the case of Meyer Prix, the customer care department was interested in the CSN but became unconvinced because of the series of rescheduled and cancelled meetings. Had the change facilitator connected with the head of customer care, he could have at least tapped into this group of CSN as a gauge of the ground sentiment.

End users or staff delegated to be in a CSN will be participative and will collaborate if given the time and/or incentive to do so. Middle managers generally have the trust of their team and are the gatekeepers to this group of people who will be impacted by change in an organization. Building a relationship with middle management in the case of Meyer Prix would have alleviated a lot of the change facilitator's frustration in accessing the group of people most impacted by change. The latter's strategy in facilitating this change would have also been more specific and targeted at the existing concerns.

Using this knowledge to strengthen change initiatives

Knowledge on the positioning of middle management will tremendously help you in assessing challenges and how best to address them. Without engaging with middle managers and building a relationship with them, it will be difficult to gain insights on their pressure points and interests. You will also definitely miss any shifts in their positioning until it is too late. Earlier sections of this chapter have proposed some typical difficulties that can arise if a strong relationship between the change facilitator and middle management is not in place. The question now, is how can that knowledge help you during a change project and when you are building your relationship with middle managers?

Facilitate with a high level of awareness

First, your new heightened awareness of how essential middle managers are for a smooth transition, will automatically guide a lot of your interactions with them. You will question any existing assumptions you have of middle managers to ensure that you are not surprised later on in the project. Seeing them in the role of gate keepers to the group of end users/staff and the creation of the CSN will keep you on your toes and remind you of the need to strategize. You will have to plan how best to gain access to the inner circle, be it through sessions on change facilitation or regular updates with them.

Incorporate guidance, support and patience in your facilitation to enable change issues to be articulated

Your role in facilitating change is not just about planning and executing a change plan. Remember to patiently offer support to middle management. Facilitating change needs a layer of guidance and support to management so that they can understand the impacts of change in an organization and are then armed to assess change difficulties they encounter.

During the implementation phase of change projects, middle managers face numerous change issues, which are often wrongly articulated as operational issues. If you have a relationship with middle management, you will be able to guide them on how to report on their change issues to top management/sponsor.

It is an important achievement for the change management path of a project when middle management start reporting on change issues.

Together, with you, they begin to put people at the center of projects.

Validation of change issues and receptiveness to your proposals

As change facilitator you will most likely be flagging change issues to the sponsor but they will be presented in a very high level view. When middle managers raise the same issues, in a more specific manner, the sponsor will not be taken by surprise but will see middle managers validating these issues. This means that top management will be more receptive to your proposed suggestions to address the change problems. Such an endorsement of middle management of the change mindset will also be reassuring for staff, who see their difficulties during a change project being highlighted to the top and being addressed. As staff start to see their organization being truly people focused, a few of their emotional resistance factors will start to disappear.

Obtaining more realistic change readiness results

Bear in mind that a change readiness assessment, carried out after a project is officially launched, will possibly give skewed results. In some countries and organizations, the culture in place will mean that after a project is launched, staff will feel they cannot be completely honest as they may be perceived as being unsupportive. As a result, the more subjective factors affecting readiness such as mindset, commitment may be skewed. In terms of capacity, there may also be existing gaps in staff abilities/training which the middle manager will be aware of but which will not be so transparent to you. This can be a sensitive topic with questions like "why was it not addressed before?" coming to the surface. If you have a good relationship with middle management, you will be able to validate the results of your readiness assessment with them and the CSN, enabling you to get a better sense of reality on the ground. Similarly, it is only through a relationship of trust that you will be able to get accurate information on existing gaps in training.

Strategies and Tools

Techniques to build a relationship of trust were shared in Chapter 5 and these can also be applied to middle management. In addition to these techniques, a good relationship building strategy relevant especially in the case of middle managers is to focus on the commonalities between yourself and middle management. Both change facilitators and middle managers need to navigate fluidly among different stakeholders. Middle managers navigate constantly between the top and bottom layers of an organization. Similarly an important part of your role as change facilitator is to navigate among sponsors, project managers, middle managers and end users.

It is known that people bond over what they have in common. This can be your opening to build a strong relationship. Share your experiences and challenges in navigating across stakeholders which middle managers will no doubt relate to. The best would be for this to happen in an informal setting. If that is not possible, then gauge the right timing in a conversation to bring up this common aspect of your role. It is important to remain honest when using this tactic. You are building a rapport with middle managers by using an aspect of both of your roles. You might have very different approaches to navigating among stakeholders and that's fine.

In fact it will be an insightful and interesting sharing experience. If you see that the person is not responding, then do not push it. They may not immediately see that their roles and yours have something in common. In that case, go back to the techniques of Chapter 5. Eventually as the relationship progresses, you will get an opportunity to bond with them over what you have in common.

"The art of life is a constant readjustment to our surroundings."

Kakuzo Okakaura

CHAPTER 7

Navigating Across Stakeholders

Overview

The strategic importance of building relationships with the project manager, sponsor and middle management was looked at in the three previous chapters. Strong relationships allow you to work more effectively to facilitate change. Inherent in the relationship model is also the aspect of navigating across stakeholders. You will constantly be moving from one stakeholder to another in your interactions with them.

This navigation among stakeholders is the process through which you will spot miscommunication, differences in how the project is perceived and diverging expectations on outcomes. You can then facilitate an alignment among stakeholders, who in turn will be more able to facilitate the change their organization is going through.

This chapter looks at how navigation skills support the execution of change facilitation plans. The previous chapters looked at the relationship model from the perspective of building relationships with the three stakeholders. Another important angle of the relationship model is the fluid navigation and connection role of change facilitators. This navigation skill set encompasses abilities such as influencing, emotional intelligence and coaching.

For the relationship model to work, in addition to the relationships which will be built with the key stakeholders, you will also need to be able to navigate among the key stakeholders, connect them and steadily move them towards an alignment. Therefore, the relationship model relies on the navigation and connection skills of change facilitators. However, at the same time, the relationship model also supports and strengthens these skills by setting them in the context of strong and positive relationships with stakeholders.

Navigating the path you have mapped

Planning for change involves activities such as assessing change readiness, conducting change and impact analysis among others to be able to formulate the change management strategy and plan. This enables you to map the path to people centric change. The big question is with the map in hand, are you able to navigate and find your way? How do you negotiate or overcome the obstacles you meet on the way?

The experience of the change journey matters

With people-centric change, the journey is as important, if not more, than the destination. In fact, the experience of the journey will affect the state of people at the end stages. An example that demonstrates the importance of the change journey occurred when a big department of a particular ministry, located in the old business quarters, decided to move to a newly built modern industrial park 30km away from its current location.

Having a traditional management style, that particular ministry did not see the benefit of engaging with people and facilitating the change journey. To them, the office change was approved by the

Government and was going to happen in any case. Therefore, issuing a communiqué to staff by comparing the old business quarters to the new office with its modern facilities, which included latest technology and infrastructure was an easy choice.

Staff lived through the transition period badly. They had transport concerns that were left unaddressed. There were rumors that the industrial park was still being developed and that the modern infrastructure was only half complete. Some older staff who were not comfortable with technology responded to the term 'latest technology' with fear. Rumors based on uncertainties and interpretations were rife. Staff lived the transition period with high levels of stress, fears and misconceptions.

Once the relocation happened, the new office was nice, modern and there was even a free shuttle operating within the industrial park. However, the negative mindset of people during transition prevented them from settling in smoothly and seeing this move as a positive one until much later. In addition, that particular ministry was heavily criticized by the public for their lack of planning during this relocation. The project manager handling the relocation was, in fact, on top of things and the relocation went according to plan without any delays. However because the communication on the move was minimal and the change process not facilitated, the journey was not well received. Even the industrial park suffered from rumors of it being only half complete, when it was actually ready on time.

Therefore the change journey is extremely important. As a change facilitator, you will need to manage this journey to make it as smooth as possible. Setting your change facilitation methodology within the relationship framework not only gives you support, contextual information and access to staff in developing your change facilitation strategy and plan but it also helps you to navigate across the key group of stakeholders which is essential during execution of your change plan. With a relationship of trust in place, it will be easier for you to act as a connection point and develop the change agility of an organization.

Facilitating change – a combined stakeholders' effort

In both public and private sector, change agility is an essential ingredient for the sustainability of the organization. Change agility is often determined by the culture of an organization, its commitment and capacity to change. While the change management responsibility remains with the change facilitator, for a truly smooth transition, facilitating change needs to be a joint stakeholders' effort. The three groups of stakeholders profiled in this book all have an important role to play in facilitating change. Do they know how to effectively do it? Part of your role as a change facilitator is to help them through that process.

The relationship framework centers around stakeholders who would in any case interact with each other. Such interactions, would be strongly influenced by the mindset and positioning of the different stakeholders. This is normal. Based on our roles within an organization, we see and operate in different frames of mind. In KDi's Change Facilitation Model, the first step is to "Reframe Change". This serves the purpose of having stakeholders move beyond their frame of mind and biases, often determined by their role. The Reframe stage enables stakeholders to have a common understanding of the change process, acknowledging that change can initially be frightening and overwhelming but when facilitated can also be empowering.

Taking stakeholders through the Reframe phase is far from easy. Conducting a workshop on how to "Reframe Change" may start that process but one workshop will not produce the needed outcome. In fact, it may seem to your stakeholders that you are sharing theoretical principles with them. Stakeholders who are focused on actions and outcomes will have an even harder time to engage in the self-reflection needed to reframe. Operating within the relationship model, you can connect with stakeholders to slowly guide them through this phase. Remember that in a change project, you are facilitating transition with every contact you have with stakeholders.

Understand the Navigation Role of the Change Facilitator Through the Three Earlier Case Studies

The three case studies looked at in this companion book each focused on one particular stakeholder group to demonstrate how the relationship model can support you in executing your change facilitation strategy and plan. The navigation role of the change facilitator may not have been so clearly visible because the focus was on how the relationship model could have made a difference in your change facilitation plans.

In Meyer Prix's case study, the lack of relationship and engagement with middle management caused the Change Support Network (CSN) to fail. In the analysis of how the relationship model could have helped, engaging with the head of operations, the head of marketing and the head of customer care of Meyer Prix is highlighted as being the key to access those staff impacted by the change. What also needs to be emphasized is the navigation skills of the change facilitator to move across these different middle management stakeholders. The ability of change facilitators to make use of their emotional intelligence and influencing abilities serves to align stakeholders towards one common objective.

Similarly in the case studies of Choco Ltd and Better Life Ltd, navigation skills of the change facilitator are essential. With Choco Ltd, it is clear that even if the change facilitator had built relationships with the project managers, he would need to tread carefully between the internal project manager and the vendor's project manager. As a change facilitator, you cannot be seen as protecting or favoring one particular stakeholder group. Moving across stakeholder openly and professionally with an alignment objective in mind is needed.

Moreover, issues raised in the three case studies focused on one group of stakeholder at a time. In reality, you will need to constantly move from one stakeholder group to another, navigating across power relationships, politics, different agendas and goals. In fact you might even have similar situations raised in the three case studies all arising within the same project.

The key message here is that with a solid change management plan in hand, you will need not only your relationships with the three key stakeholders but also strong navigation skills. These skills will enable you to move fluidly from one stakeholder group to another. Such skills will further support you to communicate effectively, lobby and guide stakeholders in order to get an alignment among them. It is essential to have stakeholders combine their efforts to facilitate change together. Such skills will also help you negotiate and overcome obstacles that you will face at various points in a project lifecycle.

Using this knowledge to strengthen change initiatives

It is clear that to execute your change plan, good navigation skills are needed. The relationship framework is built on the interactions of the change facilitator with three key stakeholders. For such interactions to result in an alignment of stakeholders working jointly to facilitate change, a relationship of trust is needed with each of the stakeholders.

The three previous chapters have focused on that aspect. It is also helpful when these three stakeholders have good relationships and trust each other. This is not always the case. There will be varying degrees of trust among stakeholders. Therefore, as a change facilitator you will need to be skillful in continuously moving from one stakeholder to another to push towards a much needed alignment, while maintaining the relationship. Abilities such as influencing, lobbying, emotional intelligence and coaching form part of the navigation set of skills.

Using adult learning principles in your interactions

Every interaction with your stakeholder is an opportunity – to build your relationship further, to listen to their needs, to influence and to coach. Transferable skills from workshop planning and facilitation can be useful in this context. Anyone planning to conduct a workshop will usually consider guiding principles such as learning preferences of their audience, the type of delivery, adopting a problem centered approach rather than content oriented, focusing on issues of immediate relevance and ensuring people know why they are learning can also contribute to your approach.

Why not apply these training principles outside of workshops to guide your interactions? Just like for a workshop, consider what learning results or outcome you are after. Do you want to raise the awareness of your stakeholder? Are you seeking an agreement from them? Or do you want them to do something? For example, in your interaction with the Change Support Network (CSN), you will be in your listener mode and act more as a mentor. On the other hand, with project managers, you may be more inclined to show them the approach you propose for a particular problem and get them to compromise and agree on the way to proceed.

Dealing with power relationships

An important challenge when navigating across different stakeholders is handling power relationships. Each project will be different from the other but one thing which exists across the board is power relationships. As a change facilitator navigating from one group of stakeholders to the other and attempting to bring alignment, you will definitely spot the different types of power in the workplace from legitimate power to connection power, referent power and so on. You will need to be careful about how you make use or engage in power relationships.

Power by itself is not bad. Depending on the way it is used, power can bring positive change. However, politics and power dynamics in the work place are inter connected and, because of the nature of your role in navigating constantly across stakeholders, you have to be cautious not to get caught in any power webs. You need to essentially be the same person when encouraging stakeholders to reframe the way they think about change and when having difficult discussions with them on what is needed for the project to succeed.

"It always seems impossible until it is done."

Nelson Mandela

CHAPTER 8

Living the Change: A Mantra We All Need to Embrace

Concluding Thoughts

This focus of this book on the three essential relationships of the change facilitator emphasizes the need for continuous navigation among stakeholders. The objective is to bring alignment on the project vision, consistent enthusiasm for project implementation and adoption of new practices. By building relationships of trust with the project manager, sponsor and middle management, the change facilitator can navigate steadily and fluidly to bridge gaps in alignment and communication. The latter is then better able to lobby, influence and convince these stakeholders to positively influence transition along the change journey.

How people experience the change journey matters enormously. Therefore, refined and strong navigation skills within the framework of the relationship model, is what you can rely on to steer an organization going through a change project to the destination point envisioned. The initial informal way upon which I stumbled into the world of change management allowed me to see how skillfully navigating across key stakeholders in a change project can make all the difference in facilitating change.

Continuous learning approach

Every change project will be different and will have something to teach you, if you remain open. A key aspect of continuous learning is self-reflection. Make sure to set some time for self-reflection at different points during the project. This will strengthen your relationship building skills and enhance your navigation skills, both essential to the relationship framework. There are some things which you may have unconsciously observed which will only become meaningful once you take time to do some introspection. Assessing whether you could have done things differently or analyzing why a particular strategy was a success will make you a more effective change facilitator.

You can adopt a self-reflective journal. For my own self-reflection, mind maps have proved to be most effective. In considering a situation where things did not work out, for example, you will want to identify the factors contributing to that particular outcome and most importantly why you think these factors were present. It becomes easy to leave this self-reflection exercise for later and end up not doing it. However, the benefits to your change projects and professional growth are so tremendous that you will want to make sure to use this tool. The best approach is to set reminders on your calendar to do this at regular intervals. Having a peer group to bounce off ideas and lessons learnt can also help.

Change is a constant

As a change facilitator your objective will be a smooth transition for the organization undergoing change. The change is usually spoken about in terms of project implementation. A project implementation schedule will be agreed upon, to which you will align your change facilitation plan. So what happens after the project is implemented?

After the go live date, once new systems or new ways of carrying out operations are in place, is the change over? The project might be over but from the staff/people's perspective, the change needs to be sustained. The adoption phase, which is the stage where people should be at the end of project implementation requires follow up and reinforcement.

People in the organization still need to be engaged and the communication line needs to remain open, especially since it is very likely that some teething problems will be faced and staff needs to be supported. Having facilitated change, during project implementation, with active communication and engagement, it would be a disaster if all of this stops because the implementation phase is completed. At the end of implementation, adoption is at a precarious stage and while the project can be considered successfully implemented, support is still needed for sustained adoption. For example, "post go-live" tasks could be added to project plans to ensure follow up happens. This could also be part of a sustainability plan, separate from the project plan. The sustainability plan would get activated once implementation is complete.

Feedback should also be gathered on the project's implementation phase and results reviewed to identify issues and capture lessons learnt. Another change readiness assessment can be carried out to see whether staff have learnt the required new capabilities, if they are confident with the new way of working and if they have any concerns. Training carried out during project implementation is often not enough as it tends to have a narrow focus, catering only to technical training on the aspect that is new.

Instead a more holistic approach that looks comprehensively at changes in skill requirements, job role and work processes is needed. Leaving training to the very end of the project can be problematic.

The best approach would be to ensure that learning happens during project implementation. This allows for a first training evaluation and subsequent fine tuning to the training to get employees at a higher level of capability readiness. Having training which goes beyond ensuring that employees know how to run the new system or new processes, mean that the employees will be able to see the big picture more clearly. For example if a project is bringing in a new system which also results in new customer service skills being needed, a service quality training might be needed for the organization to truly transform. The employee will understand that what is needed is not just to operate the new system but to adopt the full change that the project brings.

However, the reality is that it may not be possible to execute the holistic approach to training during the project implementation phase. This could be due to several reasons e.g. resource crunch or timeline pressure. In this case, after conducting the technical training, and completing the project implementation, a handover will be done to the managers. At this point managers, will be responsible for the sustainability plan and will need to monitor adoption. This is where it is essential for managers to ensure that the sustainability plan has the more holistic approach to training referred to earlier. Staff training will need to be reinforced not just on the technical change just implemented but also on the relevant support areas linked to the project's vision. Moreover, after implementation is complete, as part of the sustainability plan, the change communication plan and stakeholder engagement plan should also be updated.

When does a change facilitator exit the project?

Most contractual change management assignments end once the implementation phase is complete. However, at that point in a project lifecycle, changes still need to be sustained. This is a key message to leave sponsors and middle management with. With a good working relationship of trust, you have a better chance of helping stakeholders realize that everyone in an organization, at different levels, facilitates change. Sponsors, project managers, middle managers and staff all have a role to play in facilitating change. KDi's approach is to plan and implement change in your organization and leave you with trained change facilitators.

Journey of writing the book

My intention in writing this book was to provide a helpful resource for change facilitators, especially those new to this role. It is a resource with an easily applicable model. Whatever the industry and whatever the project, change facilitators can put it into practice and eventually customize it based on the context in which they work.

Often in our roles at work we move from one project to another without fully grasping the insights gained. Techniques of self-reflection and capturing lessons learnt can help absorb these insights. Writing this book enabled the lessons learnt at various level of the change facilitator role to be put together into a model.

It ended up being an extremely insightful journey for me. While in the process of writing this book, I continued to work on change projects and having a clearly defined relationship model, allowed me to better strategize, monitor and evaluate my relationships. On earlier projects, I was doing it partly unconsciously and partly based on previous experiences but without a clear model in mind. The advantage of using a model is the clear direction it provides along with the ability to measure and improve. In a way I was able to live the book.

The Relationship Model

A simple yet effective model, the relationship model can make a difference in your change projects. I would encourage you to go over some of your previous projects and consider how the relationship model could have helped with the challenges you faced. This book's insights can be applied to any change facilitation methodology you use. Once you recognize that with any new projects, whether it is infrastructure, process or product change, it is people who are at the center of change, then the next natural step is relationship building to reach out to the people and connect them to the change.

RESOURCES

CHANGE FACILITATOR REQUIREMENTS

The Change Facilitator will play a key role in change initiatives by meeting goals and keeping the change management plan on track. The facilitator will focus on the people side of change, including changes to business processes, systems and technology, job roles and organization structures.

The primary focus will be creating and implementing change management plans that minimize employee resistance and maximize employee engagement. The facilitator will work to drive adoption, greater ultimate utilization and higher proficiency on the changes impacting internal and external stakeholders.

Characteristics of an Effective Change Facilitator

- Thrives on diversity of challenges and routine
- Natural leadership skills, responding well to coaching
- Passionate lifelong learner
- Recognizes resistance to change in herself and others
- Models the strategies that move people to adoption
- An active listener, with the ability to synthesize complex issues
- Ability to communicate well with diverse groups
- Highly refined organizational skills
- Exceptional communication skills, both written and verbal
- Able to work effectively at all levels in an organization
- Excellent active listening skills
- Problem solving and root cause identification skills

- Strong analytical and decision-making abilities
- A team player and able to work with and through others
- Ability to influence others towards a common goal

Roles and Responsibilities of Change Facilitator

- Identify potential people-side risks and anticipated points of resistance, and develop specific plans to mitigate or address the concerns

- Conduct stakeholder readiness assessments, evaluate results and present findings in a logical and easy-to-understand manner

- Seek out and dispel rumors

- Support the execution of plans by key stakeholders

- Identify resistance and performance gaps, then work to develop and implement positive outcomes

- Apply a concerns-based change management approach and methodology

- Demonstrate solid understanding of how people go through the change process

- Create and enable reinforcement process, always celebrate success

- Work with project teams to integrate change management activities into the overall project plan

- Familiarize yourself with project management strategies and tools

- Develop a change management strategy based on a situational awareness of the details of the change and the groups being impacted by the change

- Identity and implement effective communication solutions to generate awareness

- Engage key stakeholders to build commitment for implementation

- Promote learning and development for adoption of new practices

- Develop a set of actionable and targeted change management plans – including communication plan, sponsor roadmap, coaching plan, training plan and resistance management plan

- Be an active and visible coach to organization's leaders who are change sponsors

- Create and manage measurement systems to track adoption, utilization and proficiency of individual changes

- Assist the implementation team to review progress towards achievement of objectives

Author

When Anjena Seewooruthun stepped into a Change Facilitation role with the Mauritius National Identity Scheme, she realized she had found her calling.

She provided change and communication leadership to the project, working with the Prime Minister's Office of Mauritius in her consulting role with the Singapore Cooperation Enterprise.

She has previously coordinated the operations of the Regional Multidisciplinary Centre of Excellence (RMCE), an EU funded start up regional organization working on capacity building programs for regional economic communities in the African region.

Currently a consultant with KDi Asia, Anjena is a Change Facilitator for projects in Africa and SE Asia. She has had a key Change Facilitation on-site role with the State Bank of Vietnam during its major IT modernization initiative.

With an undergraduate degree from London School of Economics and a master degree from RMIT University, she also holds a Change Facilitation certification from KDi Americas and a Training Certificate from ATD in the United States.

The author brings valuable experience from her background in public sector reform projects. She is passionate about capacity building initiatives where she sees sustainable changes as a key ingredient and a trigger for development.

www.ingramcontent.com/pod-product-compliance
Lightning Source LLC
Chambersburg PA
CBHW071521200326
41519CB00019B/6028